Through the Eyes of a Man

The Truth about College Dating Revealed to Women

Dr. Corey Guyton

Durham, North Carolina

http://www.thegenuinescholar.com

Acknowledgements

A special thanks to everyone who gave me feedback on this manuscript. This includes family, friends, and colleagues. I especially want to thank my wife Dr. Chutney Guyton for her critical feedback during the forming of this book. I would also like to thank Che' Starks, Mary Francis, Tenise Winn, Darnesha Talley, Jonisha Ealy, Dionna Thomas, Britt Hudson, Aleasha Motley, Ashley Easley, Alexus Tucker, Natalie Atkinson, Latesha Rutledge, and Tracy Roberts for their careful attention and suggestions.

Cover Design by Vedic Designs

Edited by ShaDawn Battle

THROUGH THE EYES OF A MAN:
THE TRUTH ABOUT COLLEGE DATING REVEALED TO WOMEN
Copyright © 2013 by Dr. Corey Guyton
International Standard Book Number 978-0-9833760-0-2

All rights reserved. Printed in the United States of America. No part of this book may be reproduced in any form or by any electronic or mechanical means including information storage and retrieval systems, without permission in writing from the author.

This book is dedicated with love to my beautiful Queen, Dr. Chutney Guyton, to the memory of my mother (Martha Ann Guyton), to my father (Paul Guyton, Sr.), to my sisters (Lashanda and Tracie), to my brother (Paul Guyton, Jr.), to my God-daughter (Gabriella Starks), to my extended family, to my fraternity brothers, to my friends, and to the individuals who have allowed me to mentor and inspire them. I am forever grateful for you and I love you!

Contents

My Story	7
Respect or Alienation	13
The Selection of a Woman	23
Clearly Defining Your Relationship	29
The Circle	39
The Reality of Sex	49
The Good Girls	61
Conclusions	67
Bonus: Other Things You Should Know	71

Chapter 1

My Story

Why did I write this book and why is a discussion about college dating so important to me? In order for me to properly answer this question, I will have to take you back a few years and discuss my journey of personal development. Through reading about my journey, you will gain a better understanding of why I am passionate about this topic and why I invest my time in helping young women avoid making decisions that could literally be the difference between life and death.

My Story

My journey dates back to my high school days. I was a very respectable young man and treated women with the utmost respect. Throughout my high school years, I remained a virgin and did not receive a lot of attention from the ladies. Most girls thought I was a nice guy and a great friend, but they did not see me as boyfriend material. To make matters worse, I was a little chubby and I attributed the lack of attention to my weight. I graduated high school without ever having a real girlfriend. I told myself that once I went to college, I was going to lose weight and make all the girls who did not give me any attention in high school, wish they had considered me.

As I promised myself, I lost 30 pounds during my first year as an undergraduate. The change in weight resulted in more attention from the ladies, and I gained more confidence. I went from being many girls' "friend" to the guy they wanted to date.

Toward the end of my freshman year of college, I got involved with Student Orientation. Student Orientation was a program that brought freshmen in before the start of school to help with their transition from high school to college. Being a part of Orientation gave me the opportunity to meet incoming freshmen prior to the start of school and also to "mark my territory" before anyone else. I knew that freshmen females were excited about coming to college and were intrigued by older men, so this worked out to my advantage.

In addition to Orientation, my friends and I ("The Crew") hosted the first party of the year at our apartment. We always invited freshmen to our parties and we knew they would come because I was "that guy from Orientation." This always resulted in us having the biggest parties with the most women. To make sure there was no competition, we limited the number of guys who came.

A combination of The Crew hosting some of the best parties on campus, the exposure I received at Orientation, and joining a fraternity early in my sophomore year resulted in me becoming fairly popular on campus. Overnight, I literally went from being a guy who did not get much attention to getting an overflow of it. I thoroughly enjoyed the new attention because it made up for the attention I did not receive in high school.

This newfound attention and status created opportunities for me to date multiple women. I quickly realized that I could get almost anything I wanted from women without being in a committed relationship. I felt that if I got into a relationship, it would take away from the attention I was receiving, and that was not a sacrifice I was willing to make. I went through my entire undergraduate career without ever being in a committed relationship.

During my undergraduate career, I misled a few women. Although I never stated that we would be in a committed relationship, I always showcased actions that made them think that we were. For example, I used terms of endearment such as "baby," "honey," and "sweetheart" to make them feel as if they were my girlfriends. I made sure that I chose my words carefully and stated them in a way that never officially declared that I wanted anything other than a friendship. I would say things like, "right now is not the time for me to be in a relationship, but who knows what could happen." Ultimately, my goal was to make sure that once I parted ways with a woman, she would never be able to say I did her wrong.

This behavior lasted until I got to graduate school. At this point I realized that I wanted a serious relationship. During my second year of graduate school, I opened myself up to a relationship and fell in love for the first time. I promised myself that whenever I decided to really settle down, I would be the best boyfriend ever and completely faithful to my significant other. I stayed true to this promise and was a really good boyfriend.

Then out of nowhere, my girlfriend approached me and stated that God had placed it on her heart to end our relationship. I did not understand this at the time and was really broken because I knew I was the perfect boyfriend and had made every effort to treat her like a queen. I did not want to believe that God would allow her to walk away from me, especially when I felt I was doing everything right. Completely heartbroken, I flew home to Georgia. Luckily, I had the support of my best friend, who allowed me to sleep on his couch while I coped with the breakup.

In hindsight, I knew the breakup was mandated by God and now I can say that I really appreciate her for following His guidance. Although she had no true explanation about why we needed to breakup, she knew that she had to be obedient. Over the years, I realized the breakup was one of the best things that could have ever happened to me because it is a big part of the reason I am writing this book.

At the moment my ex-girlfriend broke up with me, I realized that the pain I was feeling was the same pain I inflicted on others during my time in undergrad. My thinking about leading women on and being careless with their hearts changed drastically because prior to being hurt myself, I did not understand why women took breakups so hard. I used to have the mindset that they would eventually get over it. I promised myself that from that moment on, I would never again inflict that type of pain on anyone else.

I made a vow to be celibate for two years, and I was successful in upholding this promise. During this time, I had an opportunity to get my life back on track with God and I discovered part of my purpose in life: to empower college women to discover their value and to strive for the best in every aspect of their lives. As a result, I have begun to mentor young ladies by helping them avoid getting into situations that would cause high levels of pain. I have also taken the initiative to start helping women who are in unhealthy relationships by giving them advice and empowerment to help overcome their situations. One of the biggest rewards I have received for being obedient to God and for taking a vow of celibacy is, the beautiful queen I have found, who is designed specifically for me.

The truth is that deep down inside I was always a guy who had high values. My true identity was the respectful guy in high school who did not get a lot of attention. I created an identity in college that was phony and God allowed me to experience life so I could eventually come back and help others avoid making the same mistakes. I believe every action has consequences and God took me through a period of restoration--my two years away from dating. I am now restored and blessed, and I am making it my duty to give back to others through various avenues such as this book, personal counseling sessions, and presentations.

The Administrator

Fast forward a few years and I am an administrator at a university where I have worked for nearly four years. In this time, my passion to help women in college has increased because I see several young men doing many of the things I did to women and it hurts my heart. One of the biggest moments in my administrative career that pushed me to want to help young women even more was when I sat on a panel with undergraduate men about dating in college. A young lady in the audience asked the question, "How do men view women with whom they've slept with on the first night?" One undergraduate panel participant stated that it did not change the way he viewed those women. I was appalled by the answer because I felt it was a lie, but I gave him the benefit of the doubt. The young man seated next to me leaned over and asked me to answer the question because he said that if he answered the question truthfully, it would destroy his "game." This made me realize that college-aged men do not like to truthfully discuss these topics because they are currently "playing the game" of manipulating women and sleeping around, and revealing the truth would hurt their ability to play it.

My passion is also influenced by the fact that my office stays occupied with young women who come to vent about the way guys treat them. It is sad to say, but I see 17 and 18-year-old freshmen women who have been damaged to the point where they do not trust men at all. I cannot wrap my mind around the fact that these women are so young and are already damaged. There are also 21 and 22-year-old women who vent to me about their challenges finding a good guy because of the mistakes they made early in their college careers. These are the reasons I do what I do and why I want to help.

The Catalyst behind this Book

After continuously hearing these horrible stories and reminiscing on my past experiences, I decided to start conducting workshops and keynote speeches for women. The workshops have been extremely successful and I have been able to assist a lot of young women with their situations. The most valuable, positive feedback I received from my sessions was that I should write a book to help other college women dealing with similar situations. Most of the women felt that their friends at other institutions could really benefit from a book about college dating from a man's perspective. I really believed this was God's order for me, so I wrote the book. I hope you enjoy.

Chapter 2

Respect or Alienation

College is more than attending classes, making good grades, and graduating. It is a time when students go through developmental stages and create their social identities. For young ladies, college is a time when they are introduced to the "ultimate double standard," or the notion that men can sleep with as many women as they would like without being labeled a "hoe." Conversely, the same is not true for women because if they sleep with multiple guys, a scarlet letter is placed on their chests, thus creating the impetus behind this chapter. Four years of college can be an opportunity for you to gain respect or an opportunity for you to become alienated.

Before I get into the heart of this discussion, I would like to make it clear: I do not agree with this double standard and I do not give men a pass for sleeping around. This chapter is about helping women and not so much about telling men how they should improve. I will address men in a different publication or discussion.

It is also important to note that I am completely aware of the developmental process of young women when they enter college. The characterizations of these women are mere generalizations and do not reflect how I personally view young women in college. I realize that certain life experiences cause people to respond to situations differently, such as sleeping with men because of low self-esteem. This chapter is written to help you see how guys really function in college, because guys can manipulate you to believe that your actions are acceptable when, internally, they are thinking negatively of you. It is my contention that all women are great women, but some women make decisions that are more costly than others.

Freshman Year

Your freshman year of college is like being reborn again. Whatever you were in high school is no longer valid because you start with a clean slate in the eyes of others (except for those individuals who attended your high school). This is a time for you to do one of the following:

1. Continue the high values you had in high school and create a respectable identity;
2. Make up for any mistakes you may have made in high school, and demand the respect of your peers;
3. Develop a bad reputation by becoming overly consumed with college life, forgetting the high values you had in high school;
4. Continue making the same mistakes you made in high school, and establish the same bad reputation you had in previous years.

Different Types of Girls

From my experience, college men identify freshmen women by three distinct categories: the good girl, the set-it-out girl, and the middle-of-the-road girl.

I will give the characteristics of each category and my interpretation of how guys really perceive each group of women. My interpretations are based on a combination of my own college dating experiences, as well as the many discussions I have had with young men about dating.

The Good Girls

The good girls are young ladies who come to college and make it known upfront that they are primarily in school for their education. When approached, they carefully analyze and make men explain their intentions. They make it clear that they are not easy to sleep with and that sex is not their main priority. They are not always completely celibate but in order for them to engage in sexual relations, there must be some form of established commitment and a demonstration of this commitment through time and hard work.

In terms of prioritizing, good girls demonstrate the ability to balance school and social life. If they have school work that needs to be completed, they bypass parties and other social events to make sure their work gets done. When attending parties, they dress in clothing that reveals their natural beauty--apparel that is classy and leaves room for the imagination.

After the completion of their first year of college, good girls: (a) generally have a very low number of sex partners (between 0 - 2); (b) have had no one-night stands; and (c) have only had sexual relations with the one or two guys with whom they were in committed relationships. For these women, the two mistakes they made with these guys during their freshman year are viewed as "lessons learned," and they typically do not make the same mistakes in the future.

The Set-It-Out Girls

The set-it-out girls are young ladies who come to college and get consumed with the "college life." They are generally found at fraternity houses, athletic residence halls, and off-campus locations, chilling and drinking with upperclassmen. They like to be the center of attention at social functions and dress in ways that bring attention to their physical attributes. The term "Set It Out" is used because many times these ladies lay everything out for men, without requiring too much work from the men.

When approached by guys, these women instantly give out their phone numbers and many times will go to visit these men on the same night. Set-it-out girls may or may not have sex on the first night, but there is enough progress within the first visit to insinuate that sex is in the near future. These ladies give off the perception that they are more concerned with a guy's physical appearance and sexual performance rather than how he treats women and what he has to offer.

After the completion of their first year of college, set-it-out girls generally have a relatively large number of sex partners (5+). Most of their sexual encounters come as a result of randomly meeting guys they thought were cute and submitting to sex in a short amount of time. For these girls, after things do not go well with one guy, they generally find someone new to replace him.

The Middle-Of-The-Road Girls

The middle-of-the-road girls are young ladies who come to college and demonstrate characteristics of both good girls and set-it-out-girls. There is no one way to define these women because they could be a combination of good girls and set-it-out-girls, in that they will display characteristics of both. For instance, middle-of-the-road girls could be young women who dress very provocatively (revealing almost everything), but when approached by guys, these girls demand respect from them. Another example of these girls could be a young lady who sleeps with a few guys quickly but eventually realizes that she is being used by them; consequently, she changes her ways.

Guys' Perception of These Girls

Guys are like job recruiters looking for new employees to hire. They sit back and analyze young women during their freshman year to see how they conduct themselves. This observation is to determine which role they would like for these young ladies to play in their lives.

The Good Girls

When guys come across good girls, they immediately see them as challenges. One of the first indicators that a young lady is a good girl is her reaction when the guy tries to approach her. Men tend to approach freshmen casually because they assume these ladies are simple-minded and that it does not require too much work to reel them in. When guys approach a good girl and her response is to ignore him, or if she asks him questions about his purpose for trying to approach her, guys quickly come to the realization that they are not dealing with the "typical" freshman.

Many times men shy away from these women because they realize it would take too much work to get what they ultimately want, which is sex and exclusive access to them. These women seek relationships and most guys are not ready for relationships while in college. For a guy, settling down would limit the number of girls he could "mess" with on campus, and that is not a sacrifice he is willing to make. As a result, guys do not show these women too much attention.

The reality is, deep within, guys really respect these women. They usually consider them as being different from typical freshmen and mature for their age. In "guy conversations," men discuss how these women are the individuals they want when they are ready to settle down. These young ladies are what guys refer to as "wifey material," or the women who would become ideal wives one day.

There are some instances when upperclassmen pursue these young ladies in order to make them their girlfriends. The concept is to "catch the good ones young." This concept is similar to buying stock on Wall Street. That is, you find stock that has promise in its early stages and watch it gain value overtime.

The danger with good girls is that they sometimes develop low self-esteem due to the lack of interest from guys. They interpret the lack of attention as something being wrong with them. Many times they are lonely and as a result, they sometimes fall into the trap of doing things they normally would not do in order to fill the "loneliness" void (i.e. having random sex, dressing provocatively, seeking attention).

The Set-It-Out Girls

When guys come across the set-it-out girls, they immediately see them as women they want to have in their rooms. Set-it-out girls usually make it easy for guys, because most men do not have to do too much work to get what they want. When guys approach these women, most set-it-out girls do not put up a fight and typically give guys their numbers immediately. Sometimes these women are bold enough to start conversations and to ask guys for their numbers.

When set-it-out girls invite men to their rooms or vice versa, guys typically do not give them too much conversation. The primary goal for men is to figure out a way to get what they ultimately want, which is sex. If guys were referred to a set-it-out girl by a friend who had slept with her in the past, they usually employ the same tactics that their friend used to get her in bed. If a guy is one of the first people to have a set-it-out girl over, he will try various strategies to sleep with her. Prior to a set-it-out girl visiting, most guys have an idea that sex will occur because more than likely, a phone conversation or text message discussion about sex has already occurred. For guys, this makes the visit purposeful in that most set-it-out girls have already assured them that when they visit, sex will happen.

Guys show set-it-out girls a lot of attention when they first meet them. They invite these ladies over quite often (typically at night) and make them feel special. Sometimes guys make these ladies feel as if they are really into them and that they may desire more from them in the future.

The truth is that men see these individuals as "now" type girls. Guys feel that these ladies are temporarily useful because they satisfy their raging hormones at that moment, but most men have no intention of truly settling down with them. Many times guys approach these ladies because of their sexual history and/or from a friend's referral. Believe it or not, guys have talks about women who are perceived as "easy," and they exchange notes about how they have slept with them.

Most times, guys would never make these young ladies their long-term women, because most men prefer to settle down with women who are challenges. Many college men have extreme egos and would never settle down with girls who have slept with multiple guys on campus. Although guys may show these ladies a lot of attention early in their college career, by the time they are juniors or seniors, most men see them as old news, and there is usually a new batch of first-year students to pursue.

Middle-Of-The-Road Girls

When guys meet middle-of-the-road girls, they take their time figuring them out. When dealing with these ladies, guys may push the envelope more than they would with a good girl but less than they would with a set-it-out girl. For instance, a guy may not invite a middle-of-the-road girl over to his room for a few days so he can have phone conversations with her to determine what type of woman she may be. Once he invites her over, he may take his time becoming intimate with her. He may start out small by trying minor forms of affection like hugging, cuddling, and mild fondling. Then, he may move on to more intimate levels of affection like kissing, touching intimate spots, and even nudity. Finally, he may get to the more intimate forms of interactions, such as oral sex and intercourse. Guys take steps with these women because they are unsure of what type of girls they are and they want to make sure they make the right moves. Sometimes guys are lucky and find middle-of-the-road girls who lean more toward being set-it-out girls, yet other times they find middle-of-the-road girls who lean more toward being good girls.

Guys' interactions with these ladies will determine how they will view them. If the women are middle-of-the-road girls who lean more toward being set-it-out girls, guys end up treating and viewing them the same way they treat and view set-it-out girls. On the other hand, if they are middle-of-the-road girls who lean more toward being good girls, guys end up treating and viewing them the same way they would good girls. There are some middle-of-the-road girls who stay in the middle; they exhibit a combination of risky and reserved behaviors. This can be very confusing to guys. So in this situation, each individual guy creates his own perception of these ladies. I can honestly say that I did not want anyone who was a middle-of-the-road girl. I always wanted to settle down with a good girl.

Other Years in College

As sophomores, women have somewhat created an identity that others will use to define them. This identity is created by their actions during their freshman year. If they are viewed as good girls, they are now seen as valuable and upperclassmen may begin to approach them. Men view these ladies as valuable because they were able to go through an entire year without giving in to the pressures of college. On the other hand, good girls could continue to be overlooked and have feelings of loneliness because they are not acquiescent to the things most guys desire. If this is you, hopefully you will find inspiration in Chapter 7.

After their freshman year of college, the term "Middle-of-the-road girls" begins to fade out. Most guys have a sense of the type of women they are dealing with after the first year. Typically, the only middle-of-the-road girls at this point are either girls who were set-it-out girls who have now set standards; or, they are girls who were good girls but have decided to become more adventurous. Besides these two scenarios, most middle-of-the-road girls have been put into a category and men start treating them accordingly.

During their junior and senior year of college, most women have an established identity. The women who held their good girl status during their first two years of college will definitely be seen as "wifey material" and will have the respect of both males and females. They may begin to get attention from men who are seniors and from graduate students because they have established and confirmed that they have great self-control and are able to make good decisions.

The reality is that most good girls at this point in their educational careers do not find interest in many guys on campus. This is because they are very knowledgeable about the history of these men, and many good girls have enough self-respect to not date any of them. These ladies typically maintain their status as good girls through graduation, and once they hit the real world, they are able to attract men who are the "cream of the crop."

Women who are set-it-out girls for the first two years of college are no longer of any value to men on campus because there is a new batch of freshmen and sophomores from which guys can choose. These women are generally alienated because they have created bad reputations and sometimes this causes them to have low self-esteem, to quit school, or to not graduate. If they are able to date, they usually have to date younger men because most guys their age or older know too much about their history. These ladies typically go through major feelings of regret because they realize that guys used them during their first two years of college. They realize that most guys no longer have any interest in them and that they were only a temporary pleasure. After graduation, they are sometimes broken and have issues trusting men. This sometimes leads to trust issues in their future relationships, resulting in them pushing good men away.

My Advice

Please take this information seriously. I have had conversations with many guys who were adamant about not dating women who had a bad reputation on campus. For some men, it does not matter how you have turned your life around or how you have learned from your mistakes. Guys have major egos and hate to know that their women were once promiscuous. I highly encourage you to focus on school, graduation, and on creating your personal identity (without a man), instead of focusing on getting attention, sleeping around, and "having fun." I promise that if you focus on yourself, it will benefit you in the long run. A real man will find you and make you his queen and not his whore.

Chapter 3

The Selection of a Woman

For women on most campuses, college is the place where they realize they substantially outnumber their male counterparts. They also come to realize that finding a good man is tougher than writing a 20-page research paper. When single college women step foot on a college campus, they are bombarded with various categories of men: men in relationships, gay men, immature men, men who are known to be "no good," and unattractive men. This situation leaves only a few dateable guys from which to choose.

The small number of dateable guys on campus creates major issues for women because there tends to be a larger number of women trying to choose from this small pool of men. On the other hand, this creates the perfect scenario for guys because they have a large pool of women from which to choose. In the following section, I will try to explain how guys think about women they will possibly date. It is important for me to note here that this is also the way I analyzed women while in undergrad. Also, after discussing this method with other men, they stated that they used a similar process. Hopefully, this chapter will shed light on how guys end up with certain women.

The Woman Lot

The few guys who want serious relationships in college select their women similar to the way people select cars. Car buyers find their selection at the car lot. Guys use the college campus as their woman lot. The following chart will explain the similarities between the two:

Car Lot	Woman Lot
When customers walk onto a car lot, they see a large selection of cars.	When guys walk on a college campus, they see a large selection of women.
The first thing people think about is the year, make, and model of the car they desire to own.	The first thing guys notice on women is their exterior: particularly the way they dress, the way they take care of themselves cosmetically, and their cleanliness.
Customers ask for a Carfax report to check the vehicle's history, particularly checking for the following: · previous owners · mileage · accident history · reliability · other potential issues	Guys ask for the Womanfax report to check her history on campus, particularly checking for the following: · previous relationships (who she dated in the past) · mileage (how many people she has already slept with) · accident history (determining whether she has been wounded by past bad relationships) · reliability (determining if she will remain faithful and down for her man) · other potential issues (psychoses, drama, STDs, etc)
Customers have their credit checked to see what type of car they are capable of buying. If your credit is low, you can only afford a car with lower value, but if your credit is high, you can afford a car with high value.	Guys ask friends and associates whether they think they have what it takes to get a particular woman. This is the guy's way of doing a "credit check." If the guy has a lot going for himself, such as being smart, popular, or attractive, he realizes he has access to high quality women. If he does not possess the qualities mentioned above, or other notable characteristics, he realizes he cannot have access to certain women because his "credit" is low.

Customers often test drive cars to get a feel for how it drives, how it rides, if it handles curves well, among other things. This helps them determine whether they want to purchase the car.	Guys "talk to" and/or date women to see if they are possibly worth pursuing.
Customers consult with family and friends to validate whether they should purchase a car, or to see whether their family and friends like the car.	Guys talk to friends and sometimes family about whether they should pursue a relationship, or to see if family and friends like the woman they are thinking about pursuing.
Once purchased, customers are excited to showcase their vehicle if it lives up to their expectations. If it turns out to be a lemon (a car that looks good but does not function properly), they may try to return it. However, if kept as a lemon, they usually will not take good care of it, nor put effort into rebuilding it.	Once dating or in a formal relationship, guys are excited to showcase their women to others if they live up to their expectations. If they do not meet their expectations, they may try to end the relationship. However, if they stay in a relationship and they do not meet their expectations, they might possibly treat the women badly.

The WomanFax Report

The WomanFax report is arguably the most important aspect of this chapter. WomanFax reports are run daily and are tools used by guys to determine if they will date a woman. There is no secure way for a man to know if a woman is worth dating, but if he completes a thorough background check on her, he can discover many important things before making a decision about pursuing her. One of our biggest fears as men is that the woman we settle down with is an undercover whore and has slept with multiple guys on campus.

Previous Relationships

When guys examine a woman's previous relationships, they look for a few things, including who she dated, how long she dated these other guys, and the nature of the relationships. First, guys want to know who the woman dated because he needs to make sure that he is not getting a woman who was rejected by another guy on campus. Men hate to know that women have dated guys with status such as athletes, Greeks, and popular upperclassmen. Sometimes men perceive the women who have dated these guys as having groupie tendencies, and they think they were only with these guys for their status. Because men have egos, they cannot date these ladies in that they do not want to be seen as the guy who dates a woman who the popular guy did not want (a hand-me-down).

Second, guys want to know how long a woman dated her previous boyfriends. If she was in long term relationships, guys can overlook her having sex with these guys because it was stable and there was a formal commitment. If she has been in four relationships within a year and has had sex with all of them, guys perceive this as her not making good decisions and giving too much of herself too quickly. Typically, guys do not want these women. On the other hand, if she had three boyfriends over 6 years (averaging two years per boyfriend), guys realize that she invested in these guys, and most men acknowledge that intimacy is a normal part of the progression of a two-year relationship.

Finally, guys want to know the nature of the relationship. If a woman was a "real girlfriend" in an openly committed relationship, guys can respect this. Contrarily, if she was in a situation where she did not have a title but functioned as a girlfriend and gave a lot of herself to him, this can bother men. A man's ego will make him ask the question, Why do we have to settle down with a woman and make her our girlfriend, when the last guy got everything out of her without making her his girlfriend? Please note that most of the things that bother guys and cause them to not select women are triggered by their egos. Although this may not be fair to women and is shallow of men, it is a reality of how guys select women.

Mileage

For the purpose of this book, mileage is defined as the number of guys with whom a woman has had sex. Ideally, most guys would prefer to settle down with a woman who had no sex partners. Although guys know there are virgins in the world, they realize this expectation is almost unrealistic. Since a lot of people have already had sex upon entering college or shortly after entering college, most men try to find women who have slept with a minimal number of men.

I have participated in several panel discussions regarding college dating and the question about mileage always emerges. I always state that there is no set number of sexual partners a woman is allowed to have in the eyes of men. Each guy has a personal threshold about the mileage he will allow, but I will say that after a woman's count leaves one hand (five guys), it can become disturbing for men.

I have noticed that age plays a major factor in the number of guys acceptable for a woman to sleep with. The older she is the more lenient guys tend to be with the number of men she has slept with. I am almost sure that an 18-year-old woman having slept with more than eight guys would be disturbing to most men.

Accident History

Guys look for women's accident histories to determine if they have been damaged. The truth is that some guys think damaged women are hard to deal with and require a lot of work. Some guys are not willing to put in the work it would take to help repair a damaged woman and would rather seek women who are not damaged. There are some issues that damaged women bring to a relationship that can be a turn-off to guys. For example, women who have trust issues and overreact to minor situations as a result of being in bad previous relationships can be disturbing to many guys. Guys' big egos make them ask the question, Why do we have to expend our energy and rebuild a woman when another guy caused the damage?

Reliability

Guys check the reliability of women because they do not want to open themselves up to women who have not been faithful in the past. If a woman has cheated on a previous boyfriend, guys assume that she will cheat on them. If a woman broke up with her previous boyfriend for no valid reason, guys tend to assume that she will break up with them for no valid reason. Although men may not admit it, many of them have fragile hearts and will take every precaution to make sure they do not get them broken. This can be seen as a major contradiction to the way guys sometime treat women's hearts.

Other

Guys also check for other things during their WomanFax investigation. For instance, most guys try to determine if a woman is psychotic or filled with drama. If a woman has slashed her ex-boyfriend's tires or fought other women as a result of him, most guys assume that she will treat their relationship the same way. Guys also check to see if a woman has any diseases or STDs, or anything else that may hurt the relationship.

My Advice

I know a lot of the material in this chapter may seem like a major contradiction on behalf of men. For example, guys want women with low mileage, but have high mileage themselves. However, I encourage you to treat guys the same way they treat you. It is my belief that women should do a ManFax report on the men they are thinking about dating. Do a complete background check on guys to learn as much as you can before making a decision to invest in him mentally, emotionally, and sexually. I think a lot of women make decisions too fast without knowing much about the guys they are dealing with. It is my belief that if you do a proper ManFax report and make a decision based on the results, it will lower your chances of getting with a guy who will hurt you. I have noticed that a lot of women have red flags in their face, but disregard or ignore them and choose to pursue the relationship. By not doing a ManFax report or disregarding the results, you increase your chances of being hurt and/or damaged. Be sure to take your time and get to know a man before you invest in him; I promise it will benefit you in the long run.

Chapter 4

Clearly Defining Your Relationship

Have you ever been in a situation with a guy and did not know what to call it? On one hand, it felt like you were a couple and you played the role of girlfriend. On the other hand, when others asked you to define your relationship status, you could not. I have seen this type of ambiguity cause many hardships for college women, ultimately resulting in a negative situation for them.

From a Man's Perspective

As I have stated many times before, a large number of college men are not interested or ready to be in relationships. I will admit that men are similar to women in that they get lonely and like having companionship, but most of the time they are not interested in settling down. When I was in college my goal was to "lockdown" a female--to keep her from messing with other guys without officially making her my girlfriend.

As a fairly popular guy who excelled academically, I knew I was a hot commodity. I knew college women saw me as a "good catch" and wanted to settle down with me. What most college women did not realize was that I had no intentions of settling down while in undergrad because

I knew once I obtained my college degree, I would have access to a different set of women: those who were college graduates. Like many guys, I always wanted to settle down with a woman who was attractive, classy, had low mileage, and was educated (hence the importance of Chapter 7). In my eyes, the latter characteristic was not achievable by women until they graduated college. This is why I never officially had a girlfriend while pursuing an undergraduate degree.

It is important to understand that guys generally tell you their intentions early in the "friendship." These intentions should serve as red flags and should not be taken lightly. The problem is that many times these red flags are overlooked and women feel that a guy will eventually change over time because she believes she is the special one. For instance, I used to always preface my interactions with women by saying "right now I'm not really looking for a relationship."

From a man's point of view, this is his warning to you and he feels he is not responsible for anything negative that happens after that point because you (the woman) are completely aware of the fact that he does not want to be in a relationship. Please note that I strategically used the words, "right now," because it left women feeling that there may be a chance I might eventually become open to a relationship with them. Please do not allow yourself to become trapped by these tactics, because if a guy is really interested in being in a relationship with you, he would tell you that he is interested and you would not have to guess.

This is very dangerous for you (college women) because after stating his intentions, he could start treating you like a girlfriend by giving you attention and showing you affection. He could also start using terms of endearment like "baby," "honey," or "beautiful." Using these terms might cause you to feel as if he is making strides toward being in a relationship, causing you (the women) to open up to him mentally, emotionally, sexually, and spiritually. While we hate to admit it, most guys know that the reason women generally open themselves up is because they have an expectation that the friendship will grow into a relationship.

The problem is that many college guys are at a selfish point in their lives. Although they have no real intentions of hurting anyone, they make most decisions based on their personal desires, which are generally sexual in nature. Their decisions could also be to satisfy their loneliness by finding a companion with whom to "kick it." Doing this creates a conflict between the two individuals because while she would like to take the relationship to another level, he does not want it to be more than it has been.

When conversations begin about moving the friendship into a committed relationship, guys are fully prepared to remind women that they were specifically told upfront that a relationship was out of the question. Because I used this tactic in the past, I am a testament to the fact that many men keep this argument stored in the back of their minds, similar to the way a card player saves his trump card in a game of spades. For college men, it is not so much about "if" the conversation about getting into a relationship occurs; it is more about "when." Guys know that once sex occurs, most women will begin to express their feelings. Therefore, men have an expectation that the conversation about advancing the relationship will eventually occur.

While in college, I had no issues with women giving me titles, just as long as it was not the title, "boyfriend." Some girls identified our situations as being a "friendship," as "friends with benefits," as "talking," or as "dating." I had no problem with this because none of these titles meant that I was completely off the market and if asked by other girls, I could honestly say I was single. Actually, these titles worked in my favor because they gave me exclusive access to the women with whom I was involved. In their eyes we were working toward a relationship and this caused them to exclusively give me their time and energy. However, in my eyes, we were friends and there was no true commitment. The overall goal was to have these ladies to myself without being their official boyfriend.

For these reasons, I encourage you to really take titles seriously and fully define what type of relationship you want and/or define the type of relationship in which you are involved. Any lapse in communication could cause you to give up more of yourself to a man than he deserves without getting anything in return. Situations like these could cause you to become bitter and lose trust in men. Although you cannot control their actions, you can control the level of access you give them.

How should you approach building a relationship with a guy?

If you are interested in a guy, it is imperative that you set boundaries in the situation from the beginning and that you maintain these boundaries throughout the relationship. Realistically, you may not know what you desire from a guy when you first meet him, but throughout your journey of getting to know him, there should be constant communication about the growth of the relationship. If you do not set boundaries, you could find yourself in a situation similar to the one mentioned earlier.

Guys who really like you and really want to be in a relationship with you will clearly state that they would like to get to know you with the hopes of things eventually turning into a relationship. In these situations, setting boundaries is still encouraged because if they are not set, you may give too much too soon. Consider the following:

> You may find a good guy who treats you like a queen and the situation may look promising. You may have had conversations about getting into a relationship and he could even take you out in public. The problem occurs whenever you give everything (mentally, emotionally, and sexually) prior to being in a committed relationship. I have seen so many women express that they are in love with certain men and/or have sex with certain men prior to being in a committed relationship. The reality is that once guys are given this much access to women without a title, there is no reason why they should advance the titles in the relationship.

Food for thought: Why would a guy make you his girlfriend when he already gets everything that a boyfriend would get, without having a title? So, a title would only put him in a box. The fact that he has already had sex with you and that you have invested so much time and energy gives him enough reason to believe that you will not leave even if he does not give you a title (read Chapter 5, "The Circle," for more about this).

Steps to Take When Pursuing a Relationship

In my opinion, relationships should occur in different stages. At each stage there should be incentives--more personal access to you--for making progression. This should be similar to job promotions: the higher your rank in an organization, the more access you have to confidential information. Please realize that progression should not be achieved without hard work. So here is my proposed set of steps toward effective dating:

1. Talking – This is when you meet, exchange numbers, and talk on the phone. At this point, you probably should not be in his room or apartment, nor should you allow him to come to your room or apartment. I would encourage you to meet with him in public locations. This will prevent you from getting into risky situations. During this time you should perform a Manfax report (referred to in Chapter 3) on him and learn more about his history.

   Please do not become physically involved with him at this point. I can almost assure you that if you become intimate with him while "talking," he will not move forward with you because it was too easy and too fast.

2. Dating – After learning more about him and realizing that you would like to potentially pursue him more, you should move to the dating phase. It is very important that you make sure he realizes that you have moved to dating. You must also make sure he fully acknowledges that he is dating you. In this phase, he should be putting more energy into you exclusively and you should go on dates. Dates should not encompass him only showing up to your room or apartment at night to hang out. A guy who is really into you will not have an issue being seen with you in public. He should be walking you to class, meeting you after class, eating lunch with you, attending sports functions with you, attending campus events with you, among other things. At this point, kissing should be the furthest you should go. Setting these boundaries will force him to gain more respect for you,

despite any attempts made to go further or even if he appears to be upset.

During situations when he tries to go further, you should continuously tell him that you have respect for yourself and you do not think anything more than kissing would be appropriate. Guys who really like you for who you are will be completely fine with this and it will make them respect you more because you are probably different than most females they have dealt with in his past. Some guys will get upset and/or leave you, and you should see this as a red flag because intimacy should not be the basis for why you are dating.

After dating for a sufficient amount of time, you should begin to have conversations about progressing to a relationship. Both of you should have enough information and interactions to know if a relationship is something you would like to pursue. If it is not, then you both can part ways without you giving too much to him (emotions, the mind, or sex).

As stated earlier, there should not be any sex at this point in the relationship.

3. Once both of you have determined you are ready to become a solid couple, you should transition into an official relationship. When a relationship becomes official, you should have an expectation that others will know about your relationship. He should introduce you to the campus as his girlfriend and he should not be ashamed to be with you in public. Relationships are not meant to be a secret. There is no reason why you should not be linked as "in a relationship" with him on Facebook, why pictures of you should not be posted on his page, or why you cannot tell others about your relationship.

In regards to intimacy, I will leave it up to you and let you determine if you will allow it to be introduced into your relationship. For so many reasons, I think it is best to wait until marriage. Although these are my beliefs, I am realistic and fully understand that many college students do not wish to wait that long. At least be at this stage before you allow yourself to engage in sexual activities with him because at this point, he has made a small promise to you, the relationship, which signifies commitment and exclusivity.

On another note, if a guy tells you that he is not interested in a relationship, you should respond by saying that you understand and you will keep it strictly platonic. You should make it known that friendship does not involve intimacy, exclusivity, or spending a lot of time. I highly recommend that if it is only supposed to be a friendship, you limit the amount of time you spend with him. If you spend enough time with him and see his potential as a boyfriend, you could find yourself catching feelings for him, making it hard for you to avoid getting into a situation in which you never get a title. Remember that he stated he is not ready for a relationship, so any advances by him contradicts what he stated he wanted: a friendship.

Title Stripped, Actions Still the Same

There are situations when a guy will give a woman a title and after dating her for a while, he breaks up with her. Breaking up is fairly typical, but the issue arises when she allows him to function in the same manner as he did when he was her boyfriend. During undergrad, I never had an official girlfriend but I told a woman I was "exclusively" dating that we needed to part ways because I was not ready for a relationship. After a few days of separation, I began to do many of the things I did when we were exclusively dating, but we were no longer exclusive. I have seen so many situations that ended this way. I will illustrate how this happens in the following example.

Example

A young lady gets into an official relationship with a guy and things are going great. After dating for a while, he spontaneously approaches her and says that he is not ready for a relationship and needs some space. She tries to respect his decision and gives him the space he requests. She is completely devastated by the break-up, and as a result, locks herself in her room, does not go to class, and then her grades begin to suffer.

After about a week of separation, he, now an ex-boyfriend, begins to text her telling her that he misses her. This correspondence is much needed because she has been going through the withdrawal of not having him around. He asks her if he can come to her room to hang out and she allows him to visit because she really misses him. When he comes to visit, he shows her a lot of affection and attention. She does not ask him about getting back into a relationship because she is content with just having him around. By the end of the night, she finds herself in an intimate situation with him. She does not see anything wrong with sleeping with him because they have a history of sleeping together.

This same scenario plays out for the next few weeks, in which he continues to text, spend time, and have sex with her. Internally, she is happy to have him around, but she really desires to have her title back. When she finally gets the courage to ask him about getting back into a relationship, he reminds her that he does not want to be in a relationship, but he really wants to be friends.

Analysis

In the situation presented above, the lady really suffered because she lost her title and had to go through withdrawals as a result. Although she is content with having him around, she ultimately does not have what she truly desires, which is a relationship. This can be extremely emotionally draining for her because she was demoted from girlfriend to friend.

She has to combat many emotions. She has to deal with the fact that there is a push and pull between him being in and out of her life. She has to play the role of girlfriend and friend. She also has to manage emotions of happiness and sadness all at the same time. Dealing with these emotions creates an emotional rollercoaster that is nearly unbearable. It is even more draining for women who know they are settling but do not feel there is much they can do about it.

Conversely, the guy got everything he wanted out of the situation. He was able to get rid of his title of being a boyfriend, while continuing to get the perks. He continues to have her attention, which his possessive nature craves, because he knows that as long as she is thinking about him and investing (mentally, sexually, and emotionally) in him, she will not open herself up to another guy. He also knows that the probability of her sleeping with another guy is low because if she did, she knows that she would have little to no chance of getting him back.

On the other hand, if he becomes involved with another woman and his ex-girlfriend finds out, he does not have to feel guilty because, technically, he is single. He does not have anything to lose by sleeping with other women because he is the person who decided to leave the relationship. If he wants to regain their relationship, he knows he can come back at anytime because her actions show that she is not over him.

How to handle a problematic situation?

If you find yourself in this situation, it is important that you use your mind and not your heart. Your heart will tell you that you love him and that you need him around. Your mind will tell you that you should not be interacting with him on this level because he is not your boyfriend. It is my belief that if a guy demotes you from girlfriend to friend, he should lose all the perks that he received when he was your boyfriend. In the situation above, he did not suffer for breaking up with her. He spent a few days away from her, but he walked back into the picture as if he had not recently broken up with her. Yet, he was rewarded his privileges, instantly.

Truthfully, he will never give her a title if he continues to get the perks that he received as a boyfriend. By reinstating the title again, he would put himself in a box and would be obligated to her. Not having a title means that he has no obligation to her and he can technically do what he wants to do.

If you are in this situation, I highly encourage you to distance yourself from him. I know that you will miss him and go through withdrawals (believe it or not he is an addiction), but it is nearly impossible to go from girlfriend to friend in a short period of time, if at all. There needs to be a period where you grieve and you should be able to be mad at him for some time. If he comes back after a few days and you agree to be friends, you have lost your ability to openly be mad at him because you agreed to be friends.

Please give yourself some space from him if he breaks up with you. If not, you will risk getting caught in "The Circle" (Chapter 5) and find yourself putting your life on hold, waiting and hoping that he will get back into a relationship with you. Remember that he broke up with you for a reason. If he wanted to be in a relationship with you, he would be in a relationship with you. Do not allow him to give the illusion that he wants to be with you by hanging with you and showing you attention because as I just stated, if he really wants to be in a relationship with you, he would. Remember that you are a queen and if he does not treat you as one, find someone who will.

Chapter 5

The Circle

I have created something called "The Circle" to illustrate the psyche of a man while dating during college. When I am giving presentations at various institutions, The Circle is typically the highlight. It is my hope and prayer that this chapter helps you either avoid getting in The Circle, or gives you enough enlightenment and empowerment to get out of The Circle. Over 90% of the women who come to me for advice are caught in The Circle, and it is disheartening because their lives are put on hold for guys who do not treat them with respect. I am definitely guilty of using The Circle while in college, and I will make sure that I explain it to you in full detail because I do not want you to become a victim.

What is The Circle?

The Circle is a strategy used by men to keep women around, regardless of the circumstances surrounding their relationship. It is not only limited to official relationships. It is also used when individuals are talking, dating, or are friends with benefits.

The Circle is broken into four levels: "Sprung," "Feeling" Neglected," "Considering Leaving," and "Danger Zone."

The Circle from a Woman's Point of View

The Sprung Stage

While hanging in the student union, a young lady is approached by a young man. He tells her that he has been watching her for some time and he would like to get to know her better. He does not ask for her phone number, but asks her for her name so that he could add her on Facebook. When she gets home, she notices that the guy has added her as a friend on Facebook and has sent her a short message expressing how he really enjoyed meeting her. She responds to his message, and for the next few days they communicate via Facebook.

After a few days, she feels comfortable enough to give him her phone number. They begin having long conversations on the phone going into the wee hours of the morning. She thinks he is fun to talk to, really attentive, and she likes that he always has things to discuss during their conversations. After days of talking on the phone, she feels comfortable enough to allow him to come to her room.

As time progresses, he constantly reassures her that he is different from other guys and that he will not hurt her. From her perspective, his actions align with his words and he makes her feel special. Thus, she begins to fall for him because he appears to be the perfect catch and he is noticeably different than the other guys she has dealt with in the past. This realization causes her to let down her guard and to start opening up herself to him emotionally (telling him how much she likes him); sexually (having sex with him); and mentally (constantly thinking about him and wanting to be with him all the time). She also begins to tell her friends how wonderful he is and how she thinks he may be "the one."

The Feeling Neglected Stage

After about a month of being with him and experiencing pure euphoria, she begins to notice that he does not do many of the things he did when they first met. The duration of their phone conversations and in-person interactions begins to decline and he now appears to be busy all the time. She begins to question him about his changes and he states that there is nothing wrong and that he has been overwhelmed with school and other personal matters.

She tries to be understanding and supportive because she cares about him, but she notices that he continues to attend parties, play video games, and hang with his fraternity brothers. This causes her to become suspicious because she feels that he has time for other things but has no time for her. This ultimately leads to her feeling neglected. She begins to question herself and tries to determine what she may have done wrong to cause him to want to distance himself from her. She tries to have discussions with him about her feelings, but he states that everything is fine and that he does not see a problem. As time goes on, his actions gradually get worse, leading to constant arguments.

The Considering Leaving Stage

With the lack of attention, constant arguments, and new accusations of him cheating, she starts to seek advice from friends. Her friends assure her that she deserves better and that she should leave him. She ponders this thought for a few days. Deep within, she does not want to leave him, but she concludes that she has no other choice. At the point when she is about to leave, actually leaves, or begins to talk to another man, he steps up his game and apologizes for his actions. He tells her that he has been dealing with a lot and that he did not intend to hurt her. He assures her that he will do better and that he really wants to be with her.

Back to Sprung

She ends up giving him another chance because, in her heart, she really wants to be with him. He stays true to his promise by doing all the things he did during the Sprung Stage. Again, she feels special and appreciated, causing her to become sprung again. This lasts for about three weeks and then she begins to notice that he is starting to neglect her all over again. And so the cycle continues.

What happened?

I am sure that many of you have been in a situation similar to the aforementioned story. The woman in the story above was caught in The Circle, which is a continuous cycle. She started in the Sprung Stage, moved to the Feeling Neglected Stage, considered leaving the situation, and right before she hit the Danger Zone, she fell all the way back into the Sprung Stage, causing her to start the cycle over again.

I would like to now show you how guys process The Circle using the same scenario. Hopefully, this will prove helpful because this is exactly what I and many of my friends did to keep women inside The Circle.

The Circle from a Man's Point of View

The Sprung Stage

While hanging in the student union a young man sees a woman whom he has been watching for some time. He has asked around about her and discovered that no other guys on campus have been sexually involved with her. This is important to him because he wants to accomplish what no other guy on campus has been able to accomplish, which is being intimate with her. He approaches her and tells her that he has been watching her for some time and he would like to get to know her. He knows that she has a certain level of respect for herself so he does not ask her for her phone number since that is what every other guy does. Instead, he tells her that he will add her on Facebook.

Once he gets back to his room, he immediately sends her a message. In the message he states that he enjoyed meeting her and he hopes she gets a good night's rest. The next day he receives a response from her. He is excited because this shows him that she has some type of interest in him. They send messages back and forth via Facebook for a few days. He eventually requests that they move the conversation to the telephone.

As the conversation moves to the phone, he becomes more excited because he is one of the first guys on campus to get this close to her. He spends many hours on the phone trying to prove that he really wants to get to know her. He makes sure he says things that make her laugh and keeps discussions going to make her feel comfortable.

After he notices that she is comfortable with him, he starts making references to them possibly hanging out. He knows that he is in good graces with her so it is only a matter of time before she invites him over. After a few weeks, she invites him to hang out in her room. This is huge for him because he has been able to accomplish what no other guy on campus has accomplished.

The invitation to visit assures him that she is really beginning to like him. He knows that she is somewhat hesitant, so he constantly reassures her that he likes her and has no intention of hurting her. She tells him about the ways guys have treated her in the past and that she has a hard time trusting men. He reassures her that he is different from other guys and he proves this to her through his actions. What she does not know is that he is only making sure to do the opposite of what every other guy has done wrong to her in the past.

As time progresses, he knows that she sees him as a great catch. This is evident because she constantly tells him he is different from other guys. After a few weeks, she begins to open up to him by telling him she really likes him. She eventually becomes completely comfortable with him and allows him to sleep with her. She starts to tell him that she is constantly thinking about him. Now, he has something to brag about to his boys because he has accomplished what all of his friends wished they could have accomplished, which is having sex with this young lady.

After sleeping with her for the first time, he knows that she has crossed a line that she normally would not have crossed. He realizes that she is having internal struggles because she has allowed a guy to sleep with her without being in a committed relationship. He apologizes to her for crossing that line and makes an agreement with her to not cross it again. He reassures her that he has no intentions of hurting her so she can feel some sense of comfort. He also tells her that he does not look at her differently because he does not want her to feel as if she did something wrong.

He continues to visit and spend time with her and "by mistake," they continue to find themselves having sex--again. What she does not know is that he recognizes she has sexual urges and desires, so when he makes moves on her, he knows that it is hard for her to control these desires because she is vulnerable and really likes him. He knows that if they get intimate in any way, it would probably lead to sex. After a few times of having sex and reassuring her that he has no intention of hurting her, she becomes comfortable having sex with him. At this point, he knows that she is officially sprung.

The Feeling Neglected Stage

After about a month of having sex and spending time with her, he realizes she has really fallen for him and she has no interest in any other guys. He comes to this conclusion because she continuously tells him this. By now, he knows that she has invested too much in him to walk away, so he becomes lax when dealing with her.

Instead of spending time with her, he returns to doing the things he did before he met her. He starts playing basketball, hanging out with his fraternity brothers, playing video games, and does other things to occupy his time. Sometimes when she calls or texts him he ignores her because he feels she always wants to be with him. He answers the phone sometimes because he does not want to come off as a complete jerk. But during these conversations he tells her that he has been busy. When she asks him what has happened to cause him to change, he realizes that the easiest way to answer the question without hurting her feelings is to say "nothing is wrong." What she does not know is that deep within, he no longer sees her the same way he did when he first met her. He has accomplished everything--sexually, emotionally, and mentally--that he intended to accomplish. Truthfully, he no longer has any use for her outside of hanging out, having sex, or chilling with her when he is bored, because he does not want to be in a relationship with her.

At this point, he knows that she will do whatever it takes to try to be with him. He continues ignoring her as usual and he only visits her late at night so he can say they "spent time together." Night visits are good for him because it is a time when he can have limited conversation with her and have sex with her. She begins to question him about her feelings of neglect, but he continues to tell her that there is not a problem. He tells her that she is too sensitive. And on most occasions, this leads to big arguments. What she does not know is that the arguments are good for him because they are his justifications for leaving her room or getting off the phone. When she is finished arguing, she is in her room upset and not functional. However, when he is finished arguing, he sees it as a way to be free from her for the duration of the time they are "mad" at each other.

The Considering Leaving Stage

He knows that he has been neglecting her by not showing her any attention, talking to other girls, and by not making her feel special. He will not tell her the truth about why he has been neglecting her because he promised her in the early part of their "friendship" that he had no intention of hurting her. Inside, he acknowledges that she is a good girl, but he knows that he does not want to be with her long term. Although he does not want to be with her long term, he does not want her to be with any other guys on campus because he is selfish. In his mind, he will do whatever it takes to keep others away from her.

He can tell that she is getting to the point where she is about to break. Her friends no longer talk to him and she constantly tells him that she does not know how much longer she can deal with feeling neglected. Although she does not say it to him, he knows that she does not want to leave him because she has invested too much. When he senses that she is on the verge of leaving him, and when she tells him she is leaving, and/or starts opening herself up to talk to other guys, he knows that he needs to step up his game so he can reel her back in.

The reason he wants to reel her back in is not so much about him wanting to be with her long term; it is more so because he does not want any other guys on campus to have her. He feels that he worked too hard to get her and his ego causes him to feel as if she is his possession. For these reasons, he takes the steps to get her back.

He begins by apologizing for his actions. In order for her to take him seriously, he knows that he has to take the blame and admit to neglecting her. Because he uses her emotions as a means of luring her back in, he makes her feel pity for him by stating that he has been going through a rough time and has been really confused. He tells her that his grades have been falling, his family has been going through some hardships, and about other issues that eventually cause her to feel sorry for him. He further says that he had *no intentions* of hurting her and that if she gives him another chance, he will make it up to her.

Inside, he is fairly confident that she will take him back because he knows she has **invested too much** into him to walk away so easily. As he calculated, she gives him another chance and he takes advantage of this chance by doing all the things he did when they first met. He does these great things for about three weeks until she begins to tell him that she is falling for him again. At this point, he knows that she is sprung again and is fully invested in him. This is his cue to become lax again and start distancing himself. And so the cycle goes on and on.

Author's Advice

The Circle is very real and I have seen a lot of women get caught in it. The area outside of the *Considering Leaving* area is known as the *Danger Zone*. The *Danger Zone* is when a woman has made up her mind to leave a man and has no desire to return. A guy's primary goal is to keep his woman from making it to the *Danger Zone*. She may be allowed to flirt with the edge of the *Considering Leaving Stage*, but he will do whatever it takes to keep her from crossing over into the *Danger Zone*.

If a guy is neglecting you and is not showing you the proper respect and attention you desire, I fully advise you to leave him. Do not give him a chance to go from the *Feeling Neglected Stage* to the *Considering Leaving Stage*. I am 100% sure that during the *Feeling Neglected Stage*, you would have told him that you were unhappy and wanted for him to improve. If he could not get it right during this time, you should not waste your time with him.

What you have to realize is that the woman in the scenario met what she thought was a perfect guy. What she really saw was an alter-ego that he created to appear as the perfect guy. This creates issues because once he begins to treat her badly, she starts to reminisce about the alter-ego that he showed her when they first met. This is why when a woman goes through rough times with a man, she states that she knows he is a good man and he has been a good man in the past. The truth is that the person she hopes he gets back to was really an illusion. She lives and stays in his circle with the thought that he will eventually revert to being this perfect guy. The reality is that it is nearly impossible for him to be that perfect guy because it was not his real identity in the first place. The true identity is the guy she experienced during the *Feeling Neglected Stage*.

My ultimate recommendation is that you go through the stages I outlined for you in chapter 4 when determining if you would like to date a guy. This will be a proactive way for you to inspect him and make sure he is really interested in you for more than your physical features. Guys can only display their perfect alter-egos for so long. The problem is that many women give themselves to men so fast that they do not give the guys enough time to reveal their true identity. Please take your time ladies when dealing with men. Run a thorough ManFax report on him and make your decision based on the results.

Chapter 6

The Reality of Sex

In the words of Salt N' Pepa, "let's talk about sex." From my personal experiences and observations, sex is an extremely popular topic among college students. In fact, it appears to be more important than education. This is evident by the high levels of student attendance at campus programs focusing on topics and discussions related to sex. When I am on panels discussing academic success, the room is somewhat empty. However, when I am on panels talking about sex, the room is usually packed. For some students, sex seems to be a necessity and some cannot function without it. For others, sex is a way to "hook" and/or keep a significant other. In this chapter, I will explain the realities of sex and how it can actually be counterproductive, especially if it occurs too quickly.

The Reality

When guys first meet women, they usually notice their physical features and view them with a lustful eye. I can recall having a conversation with a few guys and we joked about how we start down and move up. That is, when we meet women, we start at their butts and then move up their bodies, eventually making it to their face. I was definitely guilty of doing this, and like a large number of guys, I always ended up viewing them with a lustful eye.

Once guys create an image in their heads about what sex would be like with a woman, they will do whatever it takes to fulfill this fantasy. Guys' intentions for pursuing sex with women are not always to be disrespectful; sometimes they are looking to fulfill their own sexual selfish desires. Additionally, there are instances when guys may pursue women with whom they are seriously interested in dating or making their girlfriend. However, when sex is introduced, everything goes down the drain and he no longer has interest in her.

Think about this scenario. You are out with a group of your closest girlfriends and you see a Gucci handbag that costs $3000. All of your friends wish they could have it. You like the bag so much that you decide you will do whatever it takes to get it. After working extra shifts and saving money for a few weeks, you raise enough money to buy it.

When you carry the bag for the first time, all of your girls admire it and you feel that you have accomplished something great! You carry it for a few weeks and after everyone has seen it, it becomes "another one of your bags." At this point you go shopping with your girlfriends again. While shopping, you see a Prada handbag that you and your friends absolutely love. Again, you do whatever it takes to get this bag. After working extra shifts and saving money for a few weeks, you earn enough money to purchase it. You carry the new bag for a few weeks and after everyone has seen it, it becomes "another one of your bags." And then this cycle continues.

When a bag becomes just "another one of your bags," you only pull it out every now and then. Eventually, you get completely tired of it and it gets stored in your closet. You refuse to give it to someone else who may value it more because you feel that it is your possession and you worked hard to get it.

Now, imagine that you are a guy and the handbag is a woman. Using this new scenario, I will explain the psyche of a college man and his desire for sex.

A guy and his friends are walking on campus and they see a girl they think is sexy. All of his friends talk about how fine she is and how they wish they could "hit it" (have sex with her). The guy finds himself lusting for her so much that he decides he will do whatever it takes to "hit it." After using some of the previously mentioned tactics for a few weeks, he eventually has sex with her.

After doing so, he goes back and tells his buddies that he "hit it." His buddies are jealous of him and acknowledge that he has accomplished what everyone else wished they could have accomplished. This causes him to feel like a king for a few weeks because she is sprung and he has access to her anytime he likes. After a few weeks of sleeping with her, the excitement of having this girl fades away and now she becomes, "another woman with whom he has had sex."

A few days later, while walking on campus with a group of friends, he sees another sexy girl. Again, all of his friends talk about how fine she is and how they wish they could "hit it." The guy finds himself lusting for her so much that he decides he will do whatever it takes to "hit it." After using different tactics for a few weeks, he eventually has sex with her. After a few weeks of sleeping with her, the excitement of having this girl fades away and now she becomes, "another woman with whom he has had sex." This cycle then continues.

When a woman becomes "just another woman with whom he has had sex," she no longer has the value that she once had. At this point, he finds a new woman to have sex with, and his old sex partner is used periodically, or whenever he is experiencing a drought. He is too egocentric and possessive to allow her to date other guys because he feels he put in a lot of work to get her, so he does just enough to keep her in The Circle.

This story was used to hopefully convey a message that once a guy has had sex with you and the lust has faded away, he no longer has use for you, nor will he see value in you any longer. Does this mean that you are no longer a good woman?--Of course not.

Here, the guy placed value on these ladies based on their physical features and his sexual attraction to them. Once sex was accomplished and he had access to their physical features, their values diminished because he had fulfilled his fantasy. Since he saw no other value in them to keep him interested, he moved on to the next woman.

Save Sex

Because of my spirituality, I am a strong believer that sex should be withheld for the person you intend to marry. Although I think this message is an ideal one, I know that it is not necessarily a realistic one, because sex is going to happen on college campuses. For those who wish to engage in sexual relations, I highly recommend that you do not introduce sex into your relationship until a man has demonstrated that he has fallen in love with your inner person.

When guys first meet women, we build up a desire for them physically and sexually, and it becomes the value we place upon them. For example, when a guy sees a woman with a nice body and a beautiful face, her physicality is all she is worth to him at that moment because that is what drew him to her. He has not had time to get to know her internally. Since this is the value placed upon her, he hangs around and shows interest in her based on this physical and sexual value. Once he engages in sex with her, her value declines because his desires have been fulfilled. This is similar to the handbag scenario. The girl wanted the handbag so badly that she did whatever it took to get it, but when she finally got it, the desire started to fade away. This concept is very important for you to know because once the value a guy places upon you begins to fade, so will his interest, primarily because he has no other reasons to value you.

If a guy is forced to get to know a woman prior to having sex with her, and subsequently falls in love with her, it is more likely that he would value her both externally (physically and sexually) and internally (mentally and emotionally). So with this scenario, if he had sex with her and his sexual desires were fulfilled, causing her sexual value to diminish, he will still value who she is on the inside, which would more than likely result in him not walking away from her so easily.

The key is to make a guy get to know you and fall for you as a person rather than what you can do for him physically or sexually. In college, there was hardly ever a time when I tried to get to know a woman if we had already engaged in sex. After engaging in sex, guys often ask the question, "Why would I waste my time getting to know her if she has already let me have sex with her?" Truthfully, once sex is introduced into the situation, many guys only want to come to your room and do things that would ultimately lead to sex. For instance, I would always request watching a movie when I went to visit a girl. Why? Because if we watched a movie it meant that we would do a minimum amount of talking, the room would usually be dark, and we would more than likely be sitting close to one another, causing things to escalate to sex even before the movie ended.

I have seen so many women use their looks and talk about how great they are at having sex as a means to attract guys. The truth is that good looking women and great sex can be replaced overnight. There are several beautiful women on college campuses and many women who are good at sex. Men do not fall in love with sex nor do they fall in love with looks. Your looks and sexual abilities will only get you so far because over time, those things will eventually diminish.

Contrarily, when a man falls in love with the internal being of a woman, he finds it hard to let go of her. When a guy finds what he thinks is a great woman, who usually has a low number of sex partners, a great personality, a bright future, and a great deal of self-respect, he will do almost anything to keep her because she is very hard to replace. In my case, I cannot see myself losing my beautiful queen because in my opinion, she is the epitome of a great woman. It took a long time for me to find her and if I lost her, I know it would be nearly impossible to replace her.

I encourage you to be a woman who has value beyond her physical features and sexual ability. If you want a great man, you have to show him that you are a woman of internal value. Please remember that this is not only about you proving yourself to a man. He must be able to prove that he has what it takes to have access to your inner being as well, including showing a true commitment to your internal value before he is allowed to experience your physical value. A man who truly values you will support you in your endeavor to abstain from sex. If you feel that you need to consent to sex to keep a man around, I can promise that this guy is not the guy for you.

After my heart was broken, I realized how painful this was and made a vow to never make anyone feel that type of pain again. I took a hiatus from dating, and upon my return to dating, I refused to have sex with anyone. When things did not work out in my attempts at dating, I felt a sense of relief. I knew the women with whom I was involved did not feel used by me because they did not sexually invest themselves in me or our relationship. I say this to say that sex should wait until there has been a proven commitment to you because if a guy leaves you for no apparent reason or even if he has a valid reason, you will not feel as if he used you for sexual purposes, because you did not give yourself to him sexually. You do not want to be the woman he can always tell others he "smashed."

Bonus – Hip You to Game

For all the ladies who have a low number of sex partners, please be careful when it comes to opening yourself up sexually. Below is a scenario that explains why I say this:

> A guy has been watching a certain girl for some time and he knows she is a great woman and seems to have a great deal of respect for herself because she does not take much crap from guys. Everyone knows that she has only had sex with two guys, and these were both boyfriends of at least two years. He has an interest in her but he also has a huge desire to be the first guy on campus to have sex with her.
>
> He approaches her in a very charming way. He is very popular, but most people do not know his personal business because he keeps his sexual escapades to himself. She knows him from his involvement in various organizations on campus and his affiliation with a popular fraternity, but she never really thought about dating him. From what she knows, he is a pretty good guy because no one knows any of his business on campus. It just appears that he is a standup type of guy.

They begin to hang out and have conversations. He asks her about her past relationships. She tells him about them, and she also asks about his past relationships. Things are going great between them and he begins to express how he is feeling her and that she is a really cool woman to be around. They begin watching movies together and each time they watch a movie, things progress. The first night they watched a movie together, they kissed. The second night they hung out and watched a movie, they felt a little more comfortable and began to fondle each other. The third night they hung out and watched a movie, they got naked but did not have sex because she said they were moving too quickly. On this particular night, he apologized to her and agreed that they had indeed moved too quickly.

The fourth night they watched a movie, they ended up getting naked a second time. Again she stopped him before intercourse. She stated that she did not want to have sex without being in a relationship, particularly because she had never done that before. He told her that he understood and he apologized. They lied in bed for a few minutes as he held her. While lying together, he began to kiss her on her neck and eventually they engaged in sex.

After sex, she began to panic because she realized she had broken a rule that she promised herself she would never break, which was having sex with someone who was not her boyfriend. She expressed her concerns to him and he held her and told her that she would be fine and that she did not do anything wrong. He apologized for his actions and told her that it was best that they never let that happen again.

After a few days, they watched another movie and eventually ended up having sex again. This time she did not panic as much and she told him that she hopes she can trust that he will not do her wrong. He makes this promise and from this point on, they begin to have sex regularly. This goes great for a while, but eventually she began to ask him about their relationship status and posed the question, "What are we?"

There are so many layers to this story that must be explained. I have seen this situation play out so many times that it sickens me. I even admit that I am guilty of this and if I had to create a name for what guys do in this situation, I would call it "turning a relationship-type girl into a friend with benefits." For any woman who has been here, I truly apologize for any man who did this to you. You do not deserve to be manipulated and used.

In this scenario, the guy realized this woman was a relationship type of girl and that she had high self respect. He knew that he was not going to have sex with her right away. He could have genuinely liked her, but like many guys in college, he did not want to be in a relationship. Since he did not want a title, he had to find a way to get what he ultimately wanted.

1. The first advantage he knew he had was the fact that not a lot of people on campus knew his personal business (keep reading this analysis to find out why). This was an advantage for him because he knew that she would not deal with him if he was a popular guy who had slept with multiple women on campus. He realized that he passed the test when she allowed him to hang out with her.

2. The next advantage he had was the information she gave to him about her previous boyfriends. She more than likely told him everything they did right and wrong. He made sure that when he was spending time with her, he did everything she said she liked and he avoided doing everything she said they did wrong. He also expressed that he was feeling her and that she was a cool woman to be around. These words made her feel great because now she knows he really likes her, but she failed to realize that he never said he wanted to make her his woman. Remember: College guys can be intentionally ambiguous for a reason. The way things are worded is extremely important because although a guy may never lie to you, he also may not give you a straightforward answer. Always make sure to get straightforward answers to the questions that you ask, and please try not to get caught up in the responses that you may want to hear.

3. They had movie nights. As I explained earlier, movie nights are the quickest way for things to escalate. The first night, there was a good chance that the only thing he wanted to do was kiss her because he did not want her to feel as if he only wanted sex from her. Each time they watched a movie he possibly had in his mind that he would try to make it a step further each time. All guys know that women will let them know when they have gone too far, so we take small steps to see how far we are allowed to go.

4. Once they got naked, he knew that sex was in the near future. The only reason she stopped him from having sex the first time was because of her values. He knew that it had nothing to do with her not wanting to have sex with him, because she allowed him to get that far. He knew that if he remained patient and continued to make her feel comfortable, she would eventually give in because she is human and has sexual desires. Just because she is a good girl with standards does not mean that she does not have sexual desires.

5. When she stopped him the first time, he apologized because he did not want her to feel like she had done something wrong. In this situation, he knew that she was probably feeling like a hoe (pardon my terminology; I am just making a point) because she allowed herself to do something that she promised herself would never happen. In his mind, he is pretty sure they will be in this situation again. He knows that she is going to think about the fact that they almost had sex when he is gone and she will have personal battles about whether she should do it.

6. The second time they were naked and about to have sex, he apologized again when she stopped him for the same reasons as before. He did this to bring about comfort but also because he knew that after a few minutes he could get her aroused again. He knew that if he started kissing her on her "spot" (she probably told him her arousal spots in a previous sexual discussion), that she would acquiesce. This time he got her aroused and things "got out of hand." At this moment he knew that she could only

abstain for so long, so his aggression with kissing and touching made her give in.

7. While panicking, he quickly reassured her that she did not do anything wrong because he knew she felt bad about breaking her rules. He made sure he told her everything would be okay because he wanted to calm her. He again apologized, making it seem like "it just happened" randomly. He made sure he said, "We cannot let this happen again." Saying "we" takes the blame off of him and makes it "their" issue, when the whole time he knew exactly what he was doing. The reality is that he pushed her to her breaking point intentionally. He knew that if she believed it was a result of them allowing things to get out of control, she would not be able to get mad at him.

8. The next time they were to come together he knew that sex would probably happen again because she has needs. He knew that she has already broken her rule, so she would be thinking, Why stop now? She tried her best to get reassurance that he would not hurt her and he could honestly agree to this because he stated that he had no intentions of hurting her, even though this is what he will ultimately do. What he did not do was promise her a relationship, which was very strategic on his part. This is why she may become a friend with benefits instead of his girlfriend.

There are some very important things to also note about this situation (you will probably be ready to kill a guy after knowing this):

1. Earlier when I stated that people did not know much about the guy's business on campus, it was because he only dealt with women similar to the woman in the scenario. He knew that women similar to the woman in the scenario had good reputations and even if he ended up doing them wrong, they would not put him on blast. This is because ladies of this caliber do not want others on campus to know that they were engaged in casual sex because it would cause others to look at them differently and possibly lead to them being called a hoe. In the end, the ladies take this as a loss and try to avoid getting into the

situation in the future. This allows him to have a free pass to go forward and to do this to other women without anyone ever knowing, yet his business remains a secret.

2. A woman who has only had sex with guys she has been in a relationship with takes pride in having a low number of sex partners. When she gets into a situation like this and has sex with a guy without being in a relationship, she will more than likely take the "friends with benefits" role if he is not willing to give her a relationship. This is because she has sexual desires that need to be fulfilled and since she does not want to add to her bed count by opening herself to new men, she typically will choose to stick with the one with whom she has already crossed the line. She does this with hopes that he will eventually make her his woman. This is why it is so easy for guys to keep a woman like this in The Circle.

Ladies, please do not fall into these traps. The scenario presented above is not the only way that guys can be manipulative, but it is an example of how the game works. If he cannot walk with you in public and tell others that you are his "one and only" woman, then he is not worthy of having you in private. I cannot stress how important it is to make a guy get to know you and fall in love with you before you open yourself up to him. The most ideal situation involves him putting a ring on your finger and marrying you before he can have the precious treasure that you were blessed to have. Some people feel they cannot wait that long and if you are one of those people, I do not judge you. However, you should know that there are consequences for inviting sex into your relationships too quickly. I am well aware of situations where sex was introduced early and it blossomed into a great relationship. I am not saying it is not possible for this to happen, but I am saying that in my experiences and from my observations, it lowers the chances of a successful relationship.

STD Tests

This is a part of the discussion that a lot of people hate to have, but it is vital that we discuss it. Sexually transmitted diseases (STDs) are very prevalent on college campuses and no one is immune to them. My first advice is that if you are going to engage in sexual activity, please have your partner tested. I have realized that a lot of people are afraid to ask others if they have been tested. My theory is that if people get defensive when you ask them about whether they have been tested, it is something triggering their defensiveness.

This defensiveness could be caused by a person knowing they have an STD, or the fact that they really do not know their status at all and are scared to find out. I know that once I got tested and knew I did not have any STDs, I was happy to get tested for anyone. The problem is that after I got tested and realized I was STD free, I decided to quit having sex and eventually met my beautiful queen, and I have been fully committed to being monogamous.

Advice

Finally, sex should not be used as a means to attract someone. Sex should not be used as a way to keep someone, and it should definitely not be the glue that holds your relationship together. Sex should be earned through hard work and commitment; sex should be a supplement to your healthy internal/spiritual connection. Sex should also be designated for the person God has created for you.

Chapter 7
The Good Girls

My heart goes out to women who do not get much attention because they are not willing to give in to the pressures of college. There are so many young ladies who stop by my office to vent about their loneliness because guys are more interested in women who are promiscuous. If you are one of these ladies, this chapter is dedicated to you. I hope that I am able to give you the comfort you need to stay strong and uphold your values.

Think about how there are some very good rappers such as Mos Def, Common, Talib Kweli, Dead Prez, and other socially conscious rappers who try to uplift the Black community through their music. Although their music has value, society does not have a major demand for these individuals, but many of the "fly-by-night" rappers get airtime on the radio. Most of the time, people who listen to these artists are individuals who are also socially conscious themselves and are able to comprehend the music.

Similarly, women who are walking a straight line do not allow themselves to get caught up in the festivities that occur on campus. These ladies have so much value and could be a huge blessing to a man, but the college environment does not have a major demand for these types of women. Meanwhile, the "fly-by-night" women who are constantly throwing themselves at men and quickly having sex are getting the "air time" (attention). This can be very frustrating for the good girls.

I know sometimes the lack of attention can cause feelings of loneliness, but I am here to deliver the good news. I like to call this good news "pay me now, or pay me later." I used to love the "fly by night" rappers when I was in my teens and early twenties. As I got older and began to mature, I started listening to the lyrics in the songs and realized that their music was garbage. As I have grown into my manhood, I have gravitated more toward the socially conscious rappers, because I have reorganized my value system and raised my music standards.

In comparison, guys are into the "fly-by-night" women while they are young and immature. As they mature and get older, their value system will begin to adjust and their standards will also increase. As the "fly-by-night" women get older, they risk guys no longer seeing value in them and it may be tough for them to find a good man. It is similar to the difference between a hit, trendy song that tops the billboards for a few weeks and a song that never makes it to the top of the billboard, but gets played for many years. In this situation, no one will want to listen to the trendy song after it has run its course, but the non-trendy song will be in demand forever and have longevity. For the women who are walking a straight line, please know that you may not be at the top of the billboards right now, but there will be men who will want you for a lifetime. Guys will only want women who are trendy and seeking the "now" attention for the time they are at the top of the billboard (which is usually the first two years of college).

Now I know there are a couple issues with the statements I made, so I will address them:

1. The above statements mean that a man can play the game and overlook a good woman early on, but when he suddenly realizes the "fly-by-night" women are not what he really desires, then he can find a woman who walked the straight line (basically have his cake and eat it too). The point I intended to make is that you may be seen as low value now, but as time goes on your value will rise. You decide if a man who overlooked you while in college should be able to have access to you when he is older and has "seen the light."

   The truth is that when you get older and people begin to see your true value, you have the power in your hands and you get to choose who you would like to date. I believe that you should get the best man possible and if that means you want a man who is a virgin or who has only had a few sex partners, then set your standards and stick to them. Never let a man feel as if he can do whatever he wants and eventually have the ability to push a reset button like nothing ever happened. Hold guys accountable for their actions and decisions. If he wanted the "fly-by-night" girls and overlooked you, then I do not feel as if he deserves to have you whenever he matures.

2. I know some of you thought I failed to mention that as some men get older, their maturity level does not increase and they continue listening to the "fly-by-night" music. The same is true for guys as they get older. They, too, continue to chase the "fly-by-night" women. I can promise you that these are not the guys you would want to be with and they are definitely not worthy of having you. The guys who will value you are guys who want women who are more than their physical features and sexual abilities. You want a guy who is marriage material. I promise that as you get older and you find a man who sees your true value, he will eventually put a ring on your finger.

The Low Self-Esteem Illusion

The lack of attention sometimes causes women to become depressed and have low-self esteem. The truth is that the low self-esteem these women exhibit is interpreted as high self-respect by others. Although I did not give much attention to women who were walking the straight line while in undergrad, I always had respect for them. I always knew I wanted to eventually marry this category of women. I have talked to so many guys who have stated that they would never date the women they were sleeping with in college. When we are in our groups discussing women, we always single out the few women we would "wifey up," and they are more than likely women who are walking the straight and narrow line. These women are not promiscuous, are focused on school, and have good heads on their shoulders.

A Guy's Analysis of Women with Self-Respect

If a woman has the ability to control herself sexually and stay focused on her academics during undergrad, we know that when she is older and goes into the real world, she will always be focused on the important things in life and will be less likely to cheat on her man. Prior to pursuing this type of woman, we know that it will take a lot for us to become acquainted with her and even longer for us to sleep with her.

We do not mind putting in the work that is required to get a woman of value and proving our sincerity to her because it is worth it. The work will pay off in the long run because we know that random guys will not be able to easily walk into the picture and take her. We have this sense of security because she has already proven to us how hard it is to get her when we were in the process of pursuing her.

Be Lonely or Broken?

When young ladies walk into my office expressing their loneliness, I ask them if they would rather be lonely or broken. I pose this question because, as an undergraduate student, graduate student, and administrator, I have noticed that a large number of women become broken as a result of dating men in college. Each time a relationship (friendship, friends with benefits, talking, dating, or whatever the title may be) ends on bad terms as a result of the guy, women are affected negatively in some form. If this cycle continuously happens, it sometimes results in these ladies not trusting men and having low self-esteem.

Every day I see the effects of being a broken woman. I see women who are older (25-30), attractive, and have established careers who cannot successfully date because they have major trust issues. This is a major issue because when they are approached by or start dating a good guy, they eventually "run" him away because they are scarred from previous relationships.

As a man who has seen many women in this situation, I do not completely fault these women for their brokenness. Men are responsible for a big part of the damage and it is not fair to the ladies who trust them to handle their hearts with care. I do think these ladies have to take some responsibility, primarily because they made choices that put themselves in situations that allowed these men to take advantage of them. Most of these mistakes are made during college when girls are young and naïve, so I pray this book helps you avoid becoming a broken woman.

    I encourage you to stay strong and stick to your values. Remember that you are a queen and queens do not let just anyone have access to them. You should demand to be respected at all times and you should treat your body like a temple. Learn to love yourself as a single woman before you let a man into your life. I always remind women that short-term gratification could lead to a lifetime of misery: STDs, brokenness, bad reputations, no degree, and many other things. Please continue to make wise choices.

Chapter 8

Conclusion

Please remember that your college years are your developmental years in that you are discovering new things about yourself every step of the way. You were designed to be a queen, but it is ultimately your choice as to whether you become one. You are princesses right now and I encourage you to avoid wasting your time on jesters (immature men) while in college. Allow yourself time to grow into the queens you were designed to be so that your king can find you. I am old school and I believe that men should find women.

Remember that real kings treat their queens like royalty. If you do not feel like royalty in your relationship, I would say that you are not dealing with a king and you may want to reconsider the relationship. I make it my duty to make sure that my queen feels like royalty every day. She is my everything and I make sure I show her through my actions and not just my words. You deserve the same royal treatment.

Words of Wisdom

God made a promise to me after I experienced my heartbreak as I explained in Chapter 1. Through prayer, He spoke into my spirit and told me that if I focused on becoming strong in Him again and if I sought to discover my true identity, He would show me true happiness. As I stated in Chapter 1, He revealed that during the years I played the game and was "popular," I was a phony who was trying to please everyone else.

The identity I created made me believe I was happy, but it was really killing me spiritually, emotionally, and physically.

After I asked God for forgiveness, I called some of the women whom I felt I misled. I apologized for my actions and asked for their forgiveness. I took a two-year sabbatical from dating and made a vow to become celibate. During my time of celibacy, there were many days of loneliness and many temptations. I stuck to the plan that God gave me and I can honestly say that He came through on His promise. He sent me a beautiful black queen who has shown me what true happiness is and I am honored to say that I have put a ring on her finger.

I know I have done some things in the past that are not commendable and I am not proud of those moments. God forgave me and after following His plan, He restored me into the man He originally intended for me to be. Now I am able to be a blessing to many young ladies and I work tirelessly to make sure they avoid getting into bad situations.

I want you to realize that there is a plan and a special person designed for you. There was no way I could have met my queen if I had not been patient and obedient. I went through many nights of loneliness during my time away from dating, but God knew I was not ready or capable of handling a relationship at that time. For many of you who are lonely and want a man, please know that this is your time to develop into the queen you are supposed to be. Your king will find you when the timing is right. I was not always ready to be a king for my queen, but I had to go through experiences to grow into one. There is a good possibility that God is working on your king as you go through school. You have to be patient and have the faith to believe that God will deliver on His promise.

Most of you reading this book are still in college and working toward your degree, which is a full-time job in and of itself. Your heart, soul, mind, and dedication should be put into your education. You are in college for a reason (to graduate) and anything else is a distraction. You need to allow yourself the opportunity to discover who you are as a person because as you age and become more mature, the things you desire will more than likely change constantly, including your standards on men.

Remember that relationships require a lot of time, work, energy, dedication and commitment. Unless your significant other is 100%

supportive of you and your educational endeavors, one variable will take away from the other. What I mean is that either your education will distract you from your relationship or your relationship will distract you from your education, and most of the time it is the latter.

"A woman without a man is not confined to anyone and has the potential to find a perfect mate; but, a woman without a degree is limited in the things she can do in life" – Corey Guyton.

Beautiful queens, this book was written out of love and I hope that it has been a blessing to you. I really and truly care for you and I hope that your king finds you. There are nearly six billion people on this planet and only one of you. This means that you are rare, unique, and irreplaceable. Rare and unique things are usually high in value, so please remember that you are highly valuable and only a few people are capable of affording you.

Apology

I have learned over the years that many times a simple apology would help some women find closure to their negative situations. The problem is that many guys are too egotistical and have too much pride to apologize and admit that they did anything wrong. This results in women being damaged and upset forever because they never got the apology they felt they deserved.

Although I am not the guy who hurt you, I would like to apologize on behalf of any man who has done you wrong. I wrote this poem after I got hurt and realized the pain I inflicted on women. I hope you can accept this poem as an apology from me on behalf of the guy who did you wrong, so that you can move forward in life and become the queen God designed you to be.

The Apology!

Dear Beautiful Queens,

We apologize for the hurt, the pain, the sweat and the tears
We apologize for the drama, the neglect, and the abuse over the years
We apologize for the lack of love, the lack of trust, the lack of affection that wasn't given
We apologize for the time you lost by trying to make us happy, instead of you just living

We apologize for the false promises we made to make you think that it was more
We apologize for not treating your body like a temple, but instead treating your body like a whore
We apologize for intentionally causing arguments and intentionally causing drama
We apologize for NOT making you our wives, but instead making you our "baby mamas"

We apologize for allowing you to be promiscuous when we knew that it was wrong
We apologize for overlooking your true beauty within, for the pleasure of seeing you in a thong
We apologize for seeing you as a piece of meat instead of seeing you for who you really are
We apologize for leaving you at a lower level instead of helping you raise the bar

We apologize to your father for taking the innocence away from his little Queen
Knowing that he's in denial about his baby growing up and thinking that she's still clean
We apologize to your mother for the hurt and pain during labor she had to endure
Her precious little girl has now grown up and we're the reason she's no longer pure

Last but not least, we apologize to our Lord and Savior for not living by His precious Word
If we would have allowed God to lead our life, none of this would have ever occurred

Sincerely,
Apologetic Men

I Love All of You and God Bless!

Bonus: Other Things You Should Know

- Once a lady dates or sleeps with an athlete or fraternity member, it will be nearly impossible to date anyone else on the team or in that organization. This can become a problem for ladies who sleep with a guy in an organization and realize that he is an idiot. If she begins to like another member of his organization who is very respectful and with whom she is more compatible, he will more than likely refuse to pursue anything serious with her because she has already slept with another member of his organization.

- Fraternity guys and athletes share notes about their sexual experiences with women. Sometimes they can appear to be interested in you, but the real reason they are approaching you is because their "brother" gave them the "scoop" on you. To avoid this, please use the information that was presented earlier in the book to make sure that he has a true vested interest in you.

- The main form of communication in relationships should be verbal communication and not text messaging. Text messaging is too informal and causes a lack of true communication when that is the primary method used in relationships. When dating in undergrad, I preferred to communicate via text messaging because it meant I did not have to be engaged in a full conversation and it also gave me the opportunity to use shorthand responses so that I did not have to give any detailed answers. Another interesting fact is that text messaging gave me an opportunity to think of the best possible responses to any questions that may have been asked. If asked a question on the telephone, I would not have had time to make up an answer and the truth would have more than likely come out.

- Secret relationships are disastrous. Any type of relationship I had with women during undergrad, I wanted to be a secret. I always convinced my "companion" that it was in our best interest to keep it on the low. Keeping the relationship a secret allowed me to interact with other women--whom I had also convinced to keep it on the low--without anyone ever knowing.

- Secret relationships also create room for other women to "mess" with your man and use the excuse that they did not know the two of you were involved, even if you know in your heart they knew.

- Logically thinking, secret relationships are secret for a reason. My question would be, "Why would someone want to keep something so special a secret?" My woman is so special to me that there is no way I could not tell others about her. Do you not think you deserve the same?

- Secret relationships mean that the relationship will be a nighttime relationship. This is great for a guy because this means three things: 1) He does not have to be seen or spend time with you during the day. 2) He does not have to take you out in public and spend money. 3) He can truthfully tell other women that he is not in a relationship.

- Finally, secret relationships mean that a guy does not have to spend a night with you because if he stayed, he would risk being seen in the morning when he left your room. This means that after sex, he can leave without having to worry about lying with you through the night. This gives him an opportunity to go home and call his other women.

www.ingramcontent.com/pod-product-compliance
Lightning Source LLC
Chambersburg PA
CBHW071413040426
42444CB00009B/2233